The Beautiful Names of God

THE
ALL~MERCIFUL
MASTER

Erol Ergün

Written by
Erol Ergün

Art Director
Engin Çiftci

Illustrated by
Hasan Eğitim

Designed by
Nurdoğan Çakmakçı

Published by Tughra Books
26 Worlds Fair Dr. Unit C,
Somerset, NJ, 08873, USA
www.tughrabooks.com

The All-Merciful Master

ISBN: 978-1-59784-223-5 (Paperback)
ISBN: 978-1-59784-202-0 (Hardcover)

Printed by Acar Basım ve Cilt San. Tic. A.Ş.

Contents

WHAT IF I STARVE ?

One afternoon, Chirpy the sparrow was flying over the hills when he looked down and noticed that hundreds of pine trees had been planted on Shepherd's Hill. Chirpy was extremely happy! He had been wishing for trees there for years because that hill had been the only bare one in the area.

"Oh, how beautiful this hill has become!" Chirpy said. Then he swooped down to say hello to the young pine trees. But all the pines were sleeping except one. Chirpy flew to that one. "Welcome, brother," said Chirpy. "I'm Chirpy. I live in the forest just over there." The little pine answered in a sad voice,

"Nice to meet you, Chirpy. I'm Greeny."

"I'd like have a chat with you," said Chirpy, "but your friends are sleeping. I don't want to disturb them. I'd better leave soon."

"No, please stay with me, Chirpy," pleaded the little pine tree. "I'm so bored."

"OK," said Chirpy. "I'd be happy to stay with you, but I think you're very sad."

"Yes," the little pine sighed. "I feel terrible."

"What is wrong?" asked Chirpy.

"It's so hard to explain," the little pine sighed again. "Let me start from the beginning. But I wonder if my story will bore you. Do you mind listening?"

"Of course not!" said Chirpy. "I like listening! Problems get easier to bear as we share them. God likes people who are willing to look for solutions to others' problems." So the little pine started to tell his story.

"They planted me in a nursery garden in a forest. I used to live in a small bag full of soil. The gardener was a nice person. Every day he would water us and air the soil. He sometimes stood us in the sun and sometimes in the shade. He cared for all of us very well. I was really happy. I used to think that I would live like that forever. Then yesterday, everything changed. All this week humans have been holding a special celebration of forests. They brought us here from the nursery garden, and I was terribly frightened. Then, a small child picked me up, kissed me, and planted me here. Everybody was cheerful. It was like a festival day. My fear turned into joy. But my joy didn't last long. A few hours later everybody left and I was all alone. Now I feel very sad."

Chirpy tried to comfort the little pine. "Why do you feel sad?

Look how beautiful your arrival has made this hill!"

"That's true," said little Greeny, "but how are we going to survive? Who is going to water us? Who is going to air the soil? Who is going to protect us from the sun's hot beams?" Chirpy started to laugh. The little pine became upset. "Are you making fun of me?" he snapped. "You don't care, of course. You can move about by yourself. You don't need to worry about hunger or thirst."

"Of course not," said Chirpy. "Making fun of someone is not nice. I'm laughing at your concerns, not you."

"Am I wrong to be worried?"

"Well," said Chirpy, "let's say you'll be free from all your worries after you find out about Him."

"About who?" asked the little tree.

"He is the One who provides nourishment for all creatures. He is God, and He is also called the Almighty. One of His other Names is the Provider. Sometimes He directly gives us our food. Other times we have to search for our food. We may even have to work very hard to find food," explained Chirpy.

"What do you mean?" asked Greeny. "Well," said Chirpy, "creatures like you are provided with their food directly but some creatures, like we birds, get their food after some effort. We have to search for it first. We can ask Earth about how this works. Let's see if he can help us. Brother Earth, can you please tell us about how God provides us with food?"

Earth was modest as always. He never talked unless he was asked. Earth joined the conversation when Chirpy invited him. "Well," he said, "your food will be given to you through me, Brother Greeny."

"Through you?" echoed Greeny. "Yes," said Earth. "I'm responsible for feeding you. I'm dark and dry but God Almighty has given me that job to do."

"Is He the One who is also the Provider?"

"Yes, exactly! He has instructed me to prepare food for living beings: human beings, animals and plants. Vitamins, proteins,

different tastes, different smells... All of these are created in different plants, and plants receive their needs such as water and minerals through me."

"But why should I believe you?"

"Why don't you just look around? You'll see that I'm telling the truth," said Earth.

Greeny looked around carefully. He noticed different kinds of trees, grass, and flowers in different colors, and Earth was feeding all of them.

Chirpy said politely, "God Almighty prepared everything that is necessary for our life. You'll get your food through Brother Earth and you'll get water through Brother Cloud. Don't be downhearted anymore, for God the Provider loves us more than we love ourselves. He set up everything we need for our life even before we were born. Plants like you are nourished through the earth and clouds; and birds like me are nourished by the fruits of plants. You'll help the clouds to carry more rain because clouds like trees a lot. Wherever there are a lot of trees

there is a lot of rain. And soil that gets a lot of rain becomes more fertile and gives you plenty of food."

Greeny became very happy. "So you mean that I'll also help other creatures?" he asked. "Yes," said Chirpy. "You'll be a big help. I'll tell you more about the other creatures later, I hope."

"That will be nice," said Greeny, "but I don't have any concerns anymore because I have learned about God the Provider. There is no need to worry."

Chirpy heard a voice calling, "Chirp, Chirp." He looked up into the sky. His mother was looking for him. "Here I am, Mommy," he called back. "All right, honey, we've been worried about you," she said. "I'm coming, Mommy." Then Chirpy said goodbye to Greeny and flew off with his mother.

Greeny was so relaxed now that he did not worry about being alone. He was not afraid of starving anymore.

HOW DID I LEARN?

Chirpy was not around yet today. It got very hot at noontime. Greeny could not stand hot weather. He called out to Earth for help, "Hey, Brother Earth!" But Earth was sleeping and he did not hear Greeny. So Greeny called out again, but it was useless. He was losing hope. How was he going to bear this hot weather? When he was in the nursery, the gardener used to move him into the shade. He looked around. Like Earth, all the other young trees were sleeping.

He was not afraid of a lack of food or water anymore. But what about the hot sunlight? "How lucky Chirpy is!" Greeny thought. "He can just fly to somewhere cool when it's hot."

A moment later he felt something cool at his feet, although the sun was still burning down on him. He felt as if his roots were being tickled. He was curious about this feeling. Then a small beetle wriggled his head out of the soil. "Hello, brother Greeny," said the beetle. "Did I bother you?"

"Not at all," said Greeny. "I was just curious about what's happening."

"I came to help you," explained the tiny creature. "I noticed that you're tired of the hot weather so I have aired the soil by wandering about in it. There were some small pockets of water under the soil. I have opened a few channels so that the water can reach your roots."

"Oh, now I understand how I got cooler!" marveled the little tree happily.

"In a little while, Brother Cloud will also arrive, and then you'll feel better under his shadow," promised the beetle.

Greeny was very pleased. "Thank you," he said. "We're just

doing our duty," said the beetle. "You should thank the One who gave us these duties."

"Does someone give you your duties to do?" asked the little tree.

"Yes, all the creatures you see around you have some duties," answered the beetle. "But how did they learn how to do their duties?" asked Greeny curiously. "All creatures learn everything from God. He is the One whose knowledge has no limits," said the beetle.

"But how?"

"Take me as an example," said the beetle. "I haven't been to any kind of school to learn my duties, but I know everything I'm supposed to do. In other words, I'm made to feel my duties."

"So, you helped me because it was one of your duties?"

"Yes, exactly. With the talent given to me I sensed that you were tired of the hot weather and I aired the soil to deliver water to you. But I didn't get these abilities by myself. I do what God wants me to do. He has written these duties in my genes. You'll learn more about genes when you grow up."

"Then why don't I have any duties Brother?" asked Greeny.

"Oh, but you do!" said the beetle. "You have more duties than I do!"

"Really? What are they then?"

"Your first duty is to grow."

"And then?"

"Why, you're even doing us a service right now without being aware of it."

"Like what?"

"I have slept under the shade of your branches for the past two days."

"Really? That's great! What else?"

"Your roots stop the rain from washing all the earth off the side of the hill. Also, you've started to produce oxygen. As you grow bigger, you'll produce more. You'll also help in several other ways."

"But how did you learn your duties?"

"As I told you before, I was taught by God. One of His Beautiful Names is the All-Knowing, which means that there is nothing that He doesn't know. He programmed your seed, too."

"Does every being learn what it needs in the same way?"

"Not really. It depends. For instance, human beings continue learning all their lives."

"Does that mean that God doesn't teach them but they get

knowledge by themselves?"

"No. Of course it is God who teaches them, too. The difference is that God has given human beings the ability to learn quite a lot, but plants and animals can learn only a very little."

Then Chirpy arrived. Greeny was very happy. "Hi, Chirpy!" he said, "I missed you so much!" Chirpy seemed tired. He perched gently on Greeny near to his trunk on the thicker part of one of his branches. Down below, the beetle slipped away quietly between Greeny's roots.

"Hi," said Chirpy. "I've been helping my mother for a few hours. You aren't bored, are you?"

"Not really," said Greeny. "I was having a talk with a beetle. Right, brother beetle?" He had not noticed that the beetle had already gone. Chirpy smiled and said, "He has already hidden under the earth." Greeny was surprised. "Why?" he asked. "He's afraid of me because birds sometimes eat beetles."

"Oh," said Greeny with interest. "But how does he know that?"

"The One who created him taught him everything he needs to survive. He didn't learn it through experience."

"Beetle was also telling me about Him. I have learned that one of His Beautiful Names is the All-Knowing. He is the One who provides the knowledge and the talents all living beings have."

"Did you learn all that from the beetle?"

"Yes," said Greeny. Chirpy looked sad. "I wish he hadn't left us, but anyway I was going to tell you about God, too. There is no limit to His knowledge. He knows everything—our thoughts, all the things we see and what that we don't see, and everything else that you can think of."

"I cannot help being filled with admiration for Him," said

Greeny. Chirpy continued, "Yes, it's impossible not to admire Him. As you know Him more, you'll love Him more, and you'll understand life better."

Chirpy was so tired he was about to fall asleep. "Let's have a rest for a little bit. Your little shadow looks so nice. I'm thinking of taking a nap for a while," he said. "I might sleep, too," agreed Greeny.

Chirpy fell asleep right away. Greeny looked at Chirpy and thought that sleeping is also a kind of blessing. "The All-Knowing is aware of us even when we are asleep," he thought. "Dear Lord who has endless knowledge! I have started to love you very much," said Greeny, and then he fell fast asleep, too.

HOW DO I LIVE?

It was very hot in the noontime sun. It was even hard to breathe. The baby butterfly was hardly able to fly, so she decided to have a rest in a cool place for a while. She noticed that the little pine tree was asleep when she flew closer to him. She looked at the other young trees. They were sleeping, too. This would be a very good place to have a rest. Greeny seemed prettier than the others, but Chirpy was sleeping in his shade. She fluttered down to perch on another of Greeny's branches. Greeny shivered and woke up. He looked around startled, but he did not see the baby butterfly.

The butterfly was embarrassed. "Sorry, Brother Pine. I didn't mean to wake you up," she whispered. "No problem," said Greeny. "I was about to wake up anyway. It's very hot today!"

"Yes, it is," said the baby butterfly. "I came to you to be protected from the hot weather."

"Where have you come from?" asked Greeny.

"I'm on a tour with my mother," said the butterfly. "I flew a bit faster to prove that I have grown up. She couldn't keep up with me. She should be here soon, though."

"But is it a good idea for you to go on a tour in such hot weather? Your body is so fragile. Aren't you affected by the heat?" asked Greeny.

"Yes, I am, but not much," answered the butterfly.

Greeny was surprised. "That's great!" he said.

"What's great?" asked the baby butterfly. "The fact that you aren't bothered by the heat. I'm not like that. I feel as if I'm going to die any minute."

"Don't think like that," said the baby butterfly. "Every being is under His protection. Look around. Look at the trees and the flowers. They're all alive, aren't they?"

"Yes..."

"Look at this tiny crocus. She is attached to life with passion. Is there any shade around her?"

"No..."

"So, do you feel you're even more fragile than she is?"

Just then, Chirpy moved. He was probably disturbed by their voices. "Ssh!" Greeny whispered. "We should speak softly. Chirpy needs to sleep."

"Alright," said the baby butterfly. She went on, "I look more fragile than Chirpy, don't I?"

"Yes, you do."

"But both of us are alive. Look at those big trees. They were also very tiny at first, and they have grown up under the hot sun."

Baby Butterfly paused for a moment, and then she continued, "I think my mother is coming. I can smell her. Mommy! Here I am!"

Mother Butterfly spotted her baby and flew towards them. "You naughty butterfly!" she exclaimed. "You left your mother behind! Brother Tree, may I rest on you, too? I have become tired of chasing my speedy baby."

"Of course," said Greeny. "But we should be quiet," he warned. "Chirpy is sleeping."

Greeny looked at the mother and baby. Both of them were very pretty. They had many colors on their wings and beautiful, symmetrical patterns.

Baby Butterfly said, "I'm sorry, Mommy. I didn't mean to make you tired. I won't do that again."

"My dear," said her mother, "I was just worried about you. You're still very small and you haven't learned how to find your way very well yet."

"You're right, Mommy. But look! My brother pine tree has been taking care of me!"

"That's all very well, but what would happen if you came across a spider's web?" asked her mother.

Greeny was curious about spiders. "What about spiders?" he interrupted. Mother Butterfly turned to Greeny. "Spiders eat butterflies and insects. They're supposed to catch us with the ability God has given to them. And we are supposed to try not to be eaten by them. God has granted us the proper equipment to be able to run away from them. Look, I'm still alive, aren't I?" she smiled.

"Oh, I was just talking about that with baby butterfly," said Greeny. "How do you protect yourself from heat? I mean, just feel the temperature today. I feel as if we're going to fry!"

"That's nothing," laughed Mother Butterfly softly. "There are harder problems in life, you know. Wait till you see the winter. Everywhere is going to be snowy and icy. You won't see anything but white."

The little evergreen tree was surprised. "Is winter much worse than summer?" he asked. Mother Butterfly paused. "I don't think 'bad' is the right word, brother," she said. "Winter and

summer both have their beauties and difficulties. Both are necessary for life. I wish I had time to tell you about them all."

"Tell me about the difficulties," pleaded Greeny. "Well," she answered, "difficulties are part of life, too. But with every difficulty comes ease. If creatures didn't survive difficulties, you wouldn't be able to see anything around you. There is One who protects all of us, God, the Greatest. He is the One who protects us from the hot sunlight during summer."

"And God protects us from the cold during winter, doesn't He, Mommy?" interrupted Baby Butterfly.

"Certainly, my dear. Everything created by Him is beautiful.

Daytime, nighttime, summer, winter,... everything" replied Mother Butterfly.

Greeny felt more relaxed now. "Is He the One who protects us from all difficulties?" he asked Mother Butterfly.

"Of course," she replied. "One of His Names is al-Rahman, which means the All-Merciful. Every creature is under His protection and mercy. The giant elephant, the small ant, even the crocus is protected by God."

Hearing her name, Crocus turned to them. "You're talking about very interesting and beautiful things," she said. "I was also very worried last winter. I started to wilt when it got really cold. My body dried up, and I was totally covered when the snow fell on top of me. But then I found out that it was warm under the earth. My roots were covered by pods. I lived like that all through the winter. When spring came, I pushed a beautiful bloom above the earth again. I don't worry anymore. I believe

that my Lord the Most Merciful will protect me again as He protected my roots last winter."

She paused for a while, her beautiful head swaying gently. "If you don't mind," she said, "I would like to tell you one more thing." The two butterflies waved their wings gently to encourage her to go on. "There was a snake lying next to me under the soil," she said. "I was scared. I had heard that snakes were harmful animals. But he said to me, 'Don't be afraid of me, Sister Crocus. I do not eat or drink anything during the winter, except some soil. I won't do you any harm.' And as he promised, he just slept all through the winter."

"That's so interesting!" said Baby Butterfly. "So that is how Our Lord protects the snake from the cold."

Mother Butterfly said, "He protects everything in a different way. He gives some creatures the ability to protect themselves. For other creatures, He arranges things so that others take care of them. For example, pets are protected by their owners."

"And babies are protected by their kind mothers, aren't they, Mommy?" said Baby Butterfly, leaning close against her mother's side. Mother Butterfly kissed her baby and said, "And let's not forget their fathers, dear."

Chirpy woke up with a flutter of his feathers. "Oof! I slept so much," he said, rubbing his eyes. Seeing that he had woken up, Mother Butterfly and Baby Butterfly flew away. Chirpy smiled, "They're getting away from me," he said. "They must have guessed that I'm hungry."

Greeny was surprised. "Why are they are running away from you?" he asked. "If they hadn't flown away, I might have eaten them. They are not bad for supper," said Chirpy.

Greeny was confused. "But God, who is the Most Merciful, protects everything. Doesn't He protect them from you?" he asked.

"He has already protected them from me."

"How?"

"God protected them by giving them the talents of intuition and flying quickly."

Now Greeny no longer feared anything. The hot weather did not bother him anymore. He smiled at Crocus. He had found a friend who was very close to him. Crocus was a very good friend. Greeny was so happy now.

WILL HE FORGIVE US OR NOT?

The other young trees were becoming jealous of Greeny. They started to criticize him.

"He's so arrogant," said one of them. "You're right," said another one. "Look at him. He doesn't talk to us."

"How can he find so many friends?" asked another one. "He talks to someone new every day."

When he overheard their conversation, Greeny became very

upset. Somehow, he had got separated from the friends he had had in the nursery. Greeny's friends had been planted on the other side of the hill, so all of the young trees around him had come from a different nursery. In fact, he longed to talk to them, but so far he had not been able to introduce himself. For this reason, he felt left out. He felt as if he was a stranger to them. He had been about to introduce himself a couple of times, but he could not gather his courage. They did not behave warmly toward him either. What should he do? He could not decide.

Greeny knew that his friend Chirpy would not come that day. He had had an accident and broken his leg. Greeny was very upset when he heard the news from Chirpy's mother. He wanted to go to his friend and say, "Get well soon." But it was impossible. Chirpy's mother said that he would be better in about a week. But how was Greeny going to wait for a whole week? He wanted to talk to Crocus, but she was still sleeping.

Suddenly a big shadow passed over him. He was startled. Then he realized that it was the shadow of a beautiful pigeon. He had never seen such a big pigeon before. Quickly, he called out to the pigeon, "Excuse me!" The pigeon tried to stop in mid air, "Did you call me?" he said. "Yes," said Greeny. "Do you want something?" asked the pigeon. "Can we chat?" asked Greeny. "I'm so bored..."

"Why not?" said the pigeon and flew downwards. His great plump body was descending towards Greeny's slender, young branches. Greeny's needles shivered with fear. "Be careful!" he said. "Don't perch on me. I'm not strong enough to hold you." The pigeon made a sudden turn and settled on the ground next to Greeny's trunk.

"I'm so sorry, Brother Pine," he said. "I was daydreaming. I know that you aren't big enough to hold me."

"It's alright," said Greeny. "What kind of bird are you? What's your name?"

"I'm a pigeon. My owner calls me Plump Pigeon," said the large bird. "And what's your name, young pine?"

"I'm Greeny," said the young tree. "Plump Pigeon is a beautiful name. Do you have an owner?"

"Yes. I'm a pet pigeon. My owner is a very nice boy. He loves me so much, and I love him, too."

"How nice. I was also planted by a nice boy. But I haven't seen him since," explained Greeny.

When the other young trees saw that Greeny was talking with a pigeon, they started to gossip about him again. "Why, he has found yet another friend!"

"It's a very strange one this time! I think he can't find anyone else to talk with!"

"Isn't he strange, too? Look at him. He doesn't really look like a proper evergreen or any other kind of tree."

"Look how he's showing off! He's talking nonsense, I bet!"

Greeny could hear what they were saying about him, but he did not want to quarrel. The pigeon frowned. "What are they talking about?" he asked. "Don't pay any attention to it," said Greeny. "They do it all the time."

"But they're backbiting!" exclaimed the pigeon. "Backbiting is a big sin. We should warn them."

Greeny thought that the pigeon was annoyed. In fact, Plump

Pigeon was not angry. He just wanted the trees to stop their bad behavior. He turned to them. "Dear friends," he cooed. "Please don't gossip. God Almighty doesn't love those who gossip."

The tallest of the young trees was already uncomfortable about what they had been doing. He had warned his friends a couple of times, but they had not listened to him. "Brother Pigeon is right, guys. You're making a great mistake. Instead of talking nicely, why are you gossiping?" One of them replied, "But he has been looking down on us." Little Greeny was surprised. "Am I looking down on you?" All the other trees shouted, "Yes, you are!"

"You're wrong, guys!" said Greeny. "There is no reason why I would look down on you. I'm just trying to get used to my new place. I have been longing to talk to you, but I haven't had a chance. You were trying to get used to your new place, too. You were feeling suffocated because of the hot weather like me. You knew that I didn't come from the same nursery as you. I thought that you left me out of your group. I wasn't sure how to talk to you. I'm just a young tree like you. Why should I look down on you? But I'm really sorry if I made you feel bad." Greeny was on the point of tears.

The other young trees were very sorry for what they had done now. "Oh, sorry, Greeny," they said. "We were unfair. Please forgive us!"

The tall young tree spoke before Greeny. "It isn't enough for him to forgive you," he said. "You need to ask for forgiveness from God first. You've been gossiping constantly. I'm not sure if God will forgive you."

The young trees became completely terrified. If God Almighty did not forgive them, what would they do? They started to tremble. All the needles on their branches rattled and shook as if there were a great wind blowing through them. They leaned towards Greeny and the pigeon and whispered, "Is it possible that God may forgive us?"

The pigeon smiled. He was very happy that they had understood what they had done wrong. "Just be aware of what you have done and ask for forgiveness. God is the Most Forgiving. He is the One who forgives our sins. He is the One who forgives a lot."

The young trees felt much happier. It was calming to know that God is the All-Forgiving. The pigeon continued, "Everybody makes mistakes. The important thing is not to be stubborn or continue to make them. Humans make a lot of mistakes, too."

When Greeny heard the word "humans," he became very excited. He was very curious about humans. "What kind of mistakes do humans make?" he asked. The pigeon answered slowly, "Good people try not to do anything wrong. They think carefully before doing anything. For example, my owner is a very nice boy. He likes to help other people. He doesn't lie. He doesn't like being lazy. He doesn't gossip. He doesn't like backbiting."

What he said made the young trees feel embarrassed again. They bowed their heads a little in shame. The pigeon immediately saw how they felt. "I didn't mean to upset you," he said. "You have understood what you did wrong and you regret it now. I hope God forgives you, too."

The trees relaxed when the pigeon said that. The pigeon continued, "What was I saying? Oh yes, I was telling you about my friend. He never says a bad word. He doesn't fight. He doesn't damage his surroundings. But you should see our neighbor's son. He's just the opposite. So nobody likes him."

"Will God forgive him?" came a soft, little voice. Sister Crocus on the hillside had woken up, and she had been listening. "Of course," explained the pigeon. "God will forgive him if he stops acting like that. If he sees what he did wrong and promises not to do it again, God will definitely forgive him. God is al-Rahim and al-Ghafur, which means He is the All-Compassionate and the All-Forgiving. He forgives all kinds of sins, big or small.

The thing is, we should be sorry for what we do wrong and try not to do it again."

Greeny felt very happy. "God is the Most Beneficent. He loves His creatures so much. He wants what is good for everybody," he said with a smile on his face.

The pigeon was very pleased that Greeny had understood. "What a good thing it is to see your sin and turn away from it," thought the pigeon. Then he spoke again to the young trees. "The best thing," he said, "is to try to avoid doing wrong. God loves those who are careful to avoid sins."

"Is it possible to find someone who has never done wrong?" asked one of the young trees. "Everybody makes mistakes," answered the pigeon. "But the important thing is not to do wrong on purpose. Whenever you notice you have done something wrong, you should be sorry, and ask for forgiveness. You should turn to God. But you should not carry on doing the same thing and thinking 'Whatever I do, God forgives me.' That is not wise."

Plump Pigeon's speech was very helpful for all of them. The young trees wanted to hear more from him. "Sorry, guys," the pigeon said. "I need to go. I'm so late. My friend will be worrying about me."

Greeny said quickly, "Can I ask you an important favor?"

"Of course."

"Do you know Chirpy? He lives in the forest across the hill.

The poor guy has broken his leg! Can you deliver my ˋGet Well Soon´ message to him?˝

˝Sure, I can. I'm going through that forest. My home is behind that hill. See you all later. Bye,˝ he said and flapped his great wings and flew away.

˝Bye,˝ called all the trees together.

The pigeon disappeared in the sky. The young trees agreed not to gossip or backbite again. Everybody was very happy. But Greeny was the happiest of all because not only had he made new friends but he had also learned how merciful and forgiving God is.

A CURE FOR EVERY ILL

Chirpy was in so much pain. His leg was hurting a lot. Sometimes he could hardly stand the pain. His mother was taking care of him. She was his only comfort. His mother kept telling him that he would recover in a week, but how was he going to live in such pain? Sometimes he got bored too. He was missing the time he spent with Greeny. He was sure that if Greeny could have walked, he would have come to visit. Was he ever going to get better? Was his broken leg going to heal? His mother was just cleaning the wound with water.

Would that be enough?

Chirpy had helped Greeny to get rid of his worries, but, he could not calm himself. His mother had gone to fetch some more water. "Hello Chirpy," he heard somebody say. He looked around and his eyes fell on a pigeon.

"Hello," said Chirpy. "Welcome."

"Thank you, little brother. Get well soon," said the visitor.

"Oh, thank you so much. How did you know about my broken leg?"

"I've just come from Greeny's place," said the pigeon.

Chirpy was excited. He had not seen Greeny for two days. He was missing him a lot. "Greeny says to get well soon," said the pigeon. "He is so sorry that you broke your leg."

"But how is Greeny doing? Is he feeling happier?" asked Chirpy excitedly.

"He's fine. Nothing to worry about. I see you love him a lot," said the wise pigeon.

"Yes, I do," said Greeny.

"I like him, too," said the pigeon. "He is very nice."

"Yes, he is. I hope I get well soon. Then I can go and visit him every day."

"Of course you'll get well. Every ill comes with a cure. Last year, my owner's parents had an accident."

"What type of accident?" asked Greeny.

"A traffic accident," answered the pigeon. "But God protected them. You should have seen their car. It was terrifying, and if you saw it you would not be able to explain how they survived."

"Weren't they injured?"

"Of course they were! Actually, they were very seriously injured. His mother broke both of her legs, and his dad broke his ribs. They suffered a lot. But after a while they got better."

"That's what amazes me," said Chirpy. "How do all those broken parts recover?"

Chirpy's family nest was at the top of a huge pine tree. The tree was listening to them carefully. He knew that it is not nice to listen to other people's conversations, but he thought in this case it might be alright since the conversation was not really private.

He wanted to answer Chirpy's question, but he did not dare to interrupt. Gathering his courage, he tried to get their attention. "Ahem, ahem!" he coughed politely. "Excuse me, but would you mind terribly if I joined the conversation?"

Chirpy was very surprised. He had lived there since he was born and he had never heard a single word from the pine tree before. His mother had said that the pine tree did not like talking a lot. "He must have something very important to say," Chirpy thought. He looked at the pigeon. The pigeon nodded. So Chirpy said, "Of course we don't mind. We would be glad."

The pine tree cleared his throat again so they could hear him clearly. "I believe," he said firmly, "that God has created a cure for every ill and created a solution for every problem. Are you wondering why I think that? I'll tell you. Last year, a coldhearted man came to me. He examined me for a while. He looked around. When he saw that there was nobody around he struck me with an axe. I started to feel dizzy. Then he hit me again from the other side. A large piece of my trunk was broken off. My sap almost stopped running through my veins. But I think the forester must have heard the sound of the blows, for I saw him running towards me blowing his whistle. The heartless  man took his axe and ran away as soon as he saw the forester. The forester became so upset when he saw what had happened to me. 'If I hadn't come on time, he would have cut down that living tree. I'll never understand why they cut down the fresh ones instead of the dead and dried up ones,' he complained. Then he took handfuls of mud from the ground, and he plastered it over my wounds. It made me feel less pain. I was very grateful to him. He saved my life. 'The One who is the Healer is going to heal your wound' he said as he left. And as time passed

I got better until I was totally healed. 'Is the Healer mud?' I thought. Then I learned. The Healer is God who created mud with healing properties. He has hidden cures in different places. Some of them are hidden in the soil, some of them are in the roots of plants, some of them are in flowers, and others are in food. In fact, medicines are made of these things."

"That's right," said the pigeon. "It's amazing how the food we eat cures us even when we aren't aware of it. And our food prevents diseases too."

"How can it do that?" asked Chirpy. The pigeon continued, "The food we eat contains lots of vitamins, and there are cures in them. God cures every illness. He does it in different ways. He has created different things and people to cure us. For example, He made

65

the forester treat the pine's wound. Also, there are some kinds of jobs which are related to God's Name the Healer, like pharmacists, doctors, nurses, and veterinarians. They treat patients in the Name of God."

While they were talking, up bounced a little grasshopper. She showed them one of her wings. "Look at this," she trilled in her high voice. "I broke this wing last week. My Lord who is the Healer healed it completely. Chirpy was delighted. "Is He going to heal my broken leg, too?" he asked. "Of course," said Plump Pigeon. "You'll be well again within a week. A couple of days ago, I scratched my chest. I didn't show it to my owner because I didn't want to upset him. I was afraid I might lose my beauty. But yesterday I saw that the scratch was gone. There wasn't even a scar."

Bouncy Grasshopper said, "Praise be to God, who has removed all sadness from us. I love Him very much. Every cure comes from Him. We just have to pray and ask for good health. He heals us in some way." Then Bouncy Grasshopper hopped away, leaping and jumping to right and left, from place to place. Plump Pigeon said with a big smile on his face, "She's always like that. She cannot stand still for more than a minute. We are all created different!"

A short time later Chirpy's mother arrived. She was so glad to see the pigeon. "Oh, Brother Plump. Welcome," she said. Chirpy was surprised. "Do you know each other?" he asked.

"Of course," said his mother. "Where do you think I bring all the delicious and healthy food we eat from?"

"Please, Mrs. Sparrow," Plump Pigeon said. "Do not embarrass me. There is nothing to say. As you know, if you tell others about good deeds they may lose

their blessing. My owner gave me the food and I've been trying to share it with you. That's all."

"Of course," said the mother sparrow. "Actually, I've just been to your place to get some medicated water."

"Did you see my owner?"

"Yes, I did. He was preparing some supper for you. He was also wondering about where you are."

Plump Pigeon turned to Chirpy. "Don't forget what I'm going to tell you now, either," he said. "The most precious blessing is our health. It's our duty to protect our health. Try to be careful not to break any of your bones again. Don't drink cold water when you're sweaty. Keep away from junk food. Always eat healthy food which will give you all the vitamins you need. The important thing is that you should benefit from the blessings of God the Healer when you're healthy. If you take care of your body and eat healthy food, you may not be sick at all, or only rarely." The pigeon paused for a second. "It's hard to leave but I need to go now. I shouldn't keep my owner waiting. He

may become sick because of worrying. Goodbye, everyone." He flapped his wings rapidly and took off.

As he flew away, he looked back. "Chirpy," he shouted, "remember that only God can remove an illness, for He is the One who created it. Don't forget to pray and ask for health from God as well as taking your medicine, OK?"

"OK," agreed Chirpy in a happy voice. "Thank you so much." Chirpy thought about how food contains healing vitamins and how God has hidden different cures in different foods. Then he started to pray. "My Lord, the Most Gracious, the Most Merciful. I ask you to provide me with a remedy and grant me good health and cure my illness so that I can fly again and tell Greeny about one of your Beautiful Names—the Healer. You are the Most Merciful of the merciful."

"Amin," said his mother to his prayer.

Chirpy cuddled up under his mother's wing. He forgot his pains. He thought, "The sweetest medicine is the warmth of a mother's embrace."

THE ALL-BEAUTIFUL

The night sky was very bright. The moon was shining like a silver coin in the sky, and the stars were twinkling prettily. Everybody was sleeping peacefully except Greeny. He was looking up at the sky and thinking about Chirpy.

As it was getting late, Greeny was feeling more downhearted. He knew that he would feel better if he fell asleep, but he could not. He thought that gazing at the sky might soothe him. He looked at the moon. It was so beautiful and so brilliant that he could not stare at it for long. He closed his eyes to rest. Then suddenly he heard a voice. "Hey! Look here."

Greeny opened his eyes to look around but there was nobody to be seen. "Hey!" the voice said again. "Look above. I'm in the sky." Greeny raised his head. All he could see was the moon.

"Hello, brother," said the moon. "I've been watching you for a long time. Is there a problem? You look so worried."

Greeny was happy to find somebody to talk to in the middle of the night. "Yes," he said. "I can't sleep. I'm thinking about Chirpy. He broke his leg and I haven't heard from him for two days."

"Don't worry. He's sleeping like a baby," said Moon.

"But how do you know?" asked Chirpy.

"Because I can see him."

"You can see him?"

"Yes, I can see many things from up here," said Moon.

Greeny was very happy to hear that. "So you can see him now, right?"

"Of course."

"How is he? Is his leg bandaged?"

"I can't see one of his legs because he's cuddling up to his mother. But he's sleeping well, so I think he has recovered." Greeny was very happy at the good news. "Thank you very much. I'm feeling better now," he said.

Then the beauty of the moon struck him again. While he was staring, Moon asked, "Why are you looking at me?"

"Because you're so beautiful. I cannot keep my eyes off you," said Greeny.

"Thank you very much," said Moon. "Yes, I am beautiful but it

isn't from me. It's from God. For He is the one who creates all beauty. He is the Most Beautiful."

"Oh, really?"

"Of course. Actually, everything created by Him is beautiful. The important thing is to be able to see that beauty. The source of happiness is the ability to be able to recognize His Beauty."

Greeny thought about God Almighty, the creator of the universe. He remembered the day when he saw the beauty of creation in the butterflies. Everything around him was marvelous. The crocus, the violet, and the begonia were beautiful. Chirpy was beautiful. Every pine tree around him was beautiful. And the beauty of the Moon...It was gorgeous.

"My dear Lord!" he prayed quietly. "Since all Your creations are marvelous, I cannot imagine how beautiful You are!"

Moon also heard his words. "What you said is true, Greeny. One of the Names of God is also al-Jamil. That means All-Gracious and All-Beautiful; One who creates beautifully. His eternal beauty is reflected by everything. Mountains, rocks, seas, flowers, bees, vegetables, fruits, animals, and humans reflect God's eternal beauty."

Greeny became excited again at hearing the word "human." "Humans, too?" he asked. "Yes," said Moon. "Humans are the most beautiful creatures. And one of them is the best reflection of God's beauty. He is the Prophet Muhammad, peace be upon him. He is the one who told people about God in the wisest way."

As well as being beautiful, Moon was talking about very beautiful things. Now, Greeny started to wonder about the Prophet Muhammad, peace be upon him. "Anyone who sees him," added Moon, "remembers God. God created everything for his love."

"You mean God created you, and the sun, and the earth...everything for his love?" asked Greeny. "Everything you see around you," agreed Moon. "The bright blue sky, the earth covered with different and colorful plants..."

Greeny was only able to see his surroundings. But he had heard about how huge the universe is. He began to think more deeply, while looking into the far distance. "So, our Lord makes all His creatures rich with His absolute beauty. My dear Lord how magnificent you are! How wonderful is everything you have created!"

Moon loved Greeny very much. As Greeny became older, he would become more beautiful. People would rest in his shade, and birds would make their nests on his branches. Everybody who saw Greeny would witness the beauty of God Almighty.

Just then, Moon saw Chirpy wake up. The little bird was looking around. "Oh, Greeny," he sighed, missing his friend.

Moon told Greeny what he had heard Chirpy say. Greeny was happy to hear that Chirpy was awake. "Please say hello to him for me, and tell him how much I miss him," Greeny said to Moon.

Moon talked to Chirpy. Greeny could hear what Moon was saying but he could not hear what Chirpy said. "He says hello, too," said Moon. "He'll come and see you tomorrow."

Greeny was delighted. Moon added, "Chirpy is praying now. He is saying the Beautiful Names of God. He prays every day."

"Praying?" asked Greeny.

"Yes, every creature prays in its own language," said Moon. "They remember God Almighty all the time."

"So, should I pray, too?" asked Greeny.

"Of course you should. But you'll learn how with time," promised Moon. But now the sun was beginning to rise so it was time for the moon to say goodbye.

"Now I'll pass on my duty to the sun," said Moon. "I'll see you later, Greeny. The sun is more beautiful than me. He will rise soon in all his beauty. He will show the beauty of God Almighty with his light."

The moon soon disappeared. The sun rose gloriously. The heat of the sun soon made Greeny relaxed. He said, "My Lord! He is the Creator, to Him belong the Most Beautiful Names. Everything in the heavens and earth glorifies Him. He is the Almighty, the All Wise. My Lord! I love you so much."

THE RULER

It was almost noon. Chirpy was feeling good. He really wanted to visit his friend Greeny today. He missed him so much. His mother had told him not to fly for a few days because of his broken leg, but he could not wait to see Greeny.

"Mommy, please, please can I go and see Greeny today?" he begged. "Well," said his mother, "if you promise to be careful and look after yourself."

"I will! I will!" trilled Chirpy and leapt off the branch into the air. He kept going for some time. It was quite difficult to fly in fact. He still had a pain in his leg. He thought about going back home, but he decided to keep his promise to visit Greeny.

After a while, he saw Shepherd's Hill in the distance. He forgot about the pain in his leg and the difficulty in flying. Out of breath, he landed at Greeny's roots. Greeny was still sleeping. Chirpy looked at him quietly and decided not to wake him up. He spent an hour resting in the shade before Greeny awoke.

Greeny could not believe it when he saw Chirpy in front of him. "When did you arrive? Have you been waiting very long for me to wake up?" he asked happily. Chirpy was very pleased, too. "It's alright," he replied. "You look very well."

"Thank you. I'm fine. You look well, too."

"Praise be to God, I have recovered. I missed you a lot."

"I missed you, too."

"I know," laughed Chirpy. "The moon told me last night. So I came to visit you today. I think the moon told you some very beautiful things last night."

"Oh, yes. I learned from him that our Lord is the source of

beauty. I also learned about our Prophet Muhammad, peace be upon him. I was planning to ask some other questions but then the sun rose, and the moon went to sleep."

"What else were you planning to ask?" said Chirpy.

"I was looking up at the sky last night," said Greeny. "Thousands of stars looked as if they were smiling. Then suddenly I had a thought, and I wanted to ask a question." Little Crocus was listening to their conversation too. She asked, "What is your question?"

"I'm planted in the ground," said Greeny, "and so are you, Crocus. You have wings to fly, Chirpy. But if you don't flap your wings, you'll fall. So, how do the objects in the sky stay up there in the air?"

"Well, they stay there by themselves, don't they?" asked Crocus in a small, puzzled voice.

"No, it isn't possible!" exclaimed Greeny.

"You're right. It isn't possible," said Chirpy. "They don't just stand still in the air. They all move at the same time. They go round and round in a big circle, and at the same time they spin."

"Do they ever crash into each other?"

"No, they don't."

"So, how does that work?" asked Greeny.

Chirpy cleared his throat and said seriously, "God Almighty is the One who controls them. He has the absolute power. But so we can understand His power a bit better we need to learn more about objects in the sky. I'd like to ask you a question. Which one is bigger, the Sun or the Earth?" Without any hesitation they said, "The Earth is bigger, of course!"

"No, that's wrong," said Chirpy. "As well as the Sun, even the stars that look so small in the sky are bigger than the earth."

Now Greeny was really astonished. "But how can that be?" he asked. "They just look smaller because they are further away," explained Chirpy.

The Sun was listening to their conversation. He was enjoying it a lot. So that he could speak to them without blinding them, he hid behind a cloud. "Hello guys," he said in a booming voice. They were all very scared. They looked around but could not see anyone. So the Sun said in a lower voice, "Do not be afraid. It's me, Sun."

They all looked up at the sky. Sun was smiling at them from behind the cloud. "I can tell you how things stay in the sky, if you wish," said Sun. "Of course!" they all said together. "We would be glad!"

In a lovely, silken voice Sun began to speak. "Let's look at Chirpy. Compare his body to his eye. What do we see? His body is bigger than his eye, right?"

"Yes," they answered.

"How much bigger is it?" he asked. Then he answered the question himself: "Maybe a hundred times bigger. Well, the size difference between the Earth and me is even bigger than that. Millions of earths could fit inside me."

They were speechless. It was too hard to imagine. Sun went on, "It's normal to be astonished by that. But there are millions of stars like me. What is more, there are stars that are even bigger than me. But we live in peace and harmony. We always keep the same distance between us. We never go into each other's space. For example, if I were to move just a tiny bit closer to Earth, God forbid, you would all burn to ashes. Look at you now. Even though I'm hiding behind a cloud, I'm still so bright that you cannot look straight at me."

Greeny could not wait to find out more. "So who rules you?" he asked. "Who keeps this perfect system going? Who stops you from crashing into each other? How do you keep your distance the same all the time?" Sun smiled at Greeny. "You'll have to

ask Chirpy those questions," he said. "That's all from me for now."

With that, Sun hid himself completely behind the cloud and the air became cooler. Now Sun was gone, Crocus and Greeny were looking at Chirpy. They were waiting excitedly to hear from him. Chirpy paused to plan what he would say and then began. "Greeny is right," he said. "There must be someone who controls this perfect harmony between all the stars and the planets. If there were no rules and nobody in charge, what would happen?"

He answered his own question: "There would be lots of accidents, of course. When humans drive cars and trucks on their roads, accidents happen all the time. But there are no crashes between the planets, or I have never heard or seen one. Have you ever heard any?"

Crocus said happily, "I don't think so. Accidents don't happen in the sky. So God must be the Ruler who controls it all."

THE GIVER OF LIFE

Plump Pigeon was flying around. The weather was beautiful, and he wanted to spend his time wisely. As he was flying in the sky, he was observing the environment. The earth was rich with colorful flowers and green grass. The rivers were flowing smoothly. The lovely butterflies and hardworking honeybees were flying busily. Wherever he looked he was amazed by another beautiful sight.

After a while Plump Pigeon saw the tree where Chirpy's nest was. He flew closer to the tree but nobody was in the nest.

He settled on a branch to wait. Soon, he heard a small voice. "Hello," it said.

Looking around to see where the voice was coming from, he spotted Zippy Squirrel. "Hello, Zippy," he said. "What are you doing here?"

"I was going to ask you the same question, Plump," laughed Zippy. "I was just wandering around. I wanted to say hello when I saw you. I guess you're waiting for Chirpy and his mother."

"Yes,"

"I saw them near the river," said Zippy. "They were having a bath. They should come home soon. Would you like some walnut?" he offered, holding a piece out to Plump Pigeon in his paw.

"Oh, thank you very much. But I've just had lunch," said the pigeon politely.

Zippy Squirrel started to eat greedily. Plump Pigeon was watching him. When Zippy realized that, he felt embarrassed. He

knew that he should have eaten more slowly and politely. His
mother was always warning him. Unfortunately, he kept making
the same mistake. He promised himself that he would change
his habit as soon as possible.

Just at that moment, Chirpy arrived. He was very glad to see them. "Welcome," he said. "I'm so happy to see you."

"I'm pleased to see you, too. How are you?" said Plump Pigeon. "But where is your mother?"

"I'm fine, thanks, and my mother is collecting some food. She'll be here later. How are you?"

"I'm fine, too, thanks."

Zippy said, "The weather is very good today."

"Yes, that's why we went for a bath in the river," said Chirpy. "The water is very warm. If you want to, we can go again." In fact, Plump Pigeon was thinking the same thing. "That's a good idea," he said. "Would you like to come with us, Zippy?"

"I need to pick some more walnuts," said Zippy. "Maybe I'll come later."

"Oh, alright," said Plump Pigeon, and he continued, "We live in a beautiful, colorful environment. Everything is so alive."

"Yes, I was watching the fish today," said Zippy. "They were all playing together. It was very exciting. What is more, there are millions of living things on Earth. How does that happen? I can't understand it. For example, eggs are very hard on the outside but watery inside, and baby chicks come out of them. The dry trees of winter come to life again in spring. Then the black soil is covered with colorful plants. Flowers, trees, and

grass become greener. Is it possible to understand how these things happen?"

Zippy showed them what he was holding in his tiny paw. "Does anyone know what it is?"

Plump Pigeon answered, "Everybody knows what it is! It's a sunflower seed."

"Oh, yes," agreed Chirpy. So Zippy Squirrel asked, "Do you think that it's alive?" Plump Pigeon said, "Of course it isn't alive." Zippy turned to Chirpy. "What do you think, Chirpy?"

"I agree. It isn't alive."

Zippy smiled and said, "I used to think the same, but a couple of months ago, I hid a tiny seed under a small rock. I was planning to save it to eat later. But after a while, I saw that the tiny seed had come to life and started to grow. Then it grew into a tall sunflower."

A nearby sunflower was listening to them. "Zippy is telling the truth," she said. "I don't know how I got here, either. I'm supposed to grow in a field. I was bored at first, but now I'm used to being here." She carefully turned her face to the sun, then continued, "I am sorry. I can't keep my eyes off the sun. That's why they call me a sunflower. As Zippy told you before, I was just a tiny, dry seed at first. It was as if I was sleeping. Then I woke up by the command of God Almighty and grew into a tall, beautiful plant. Most things happen like that in nature. Seeds look as if they aren't alive at first. It's as if they're sleeping, but almost all the flowers and trees that we see around us come from seeds."

Chirpy asked excitedly, "How does it happen? Who gives life to those seeds?"

"Maybe they give it to themselves. Who else can it be?" asked Zippy. But Plump Pigeon said, "No, nothing happens by itself."

"So, how then?" Zippy wanted to know.

"Let me tell you," said Plump Pigeon. "My mother told me this a long time ago. One of the Names of God is the Giver of Life al-Muhyi. Every living thing gets life from God Almighty. Planted seeds come to life in the Name of God. God is the One who gives life to eggs. Baby chicks hatch out of eggs by the command of God."

Chirpy said, "I should have thought of that. Can there be life without the source of life? There are billions of creatures in the universe. Only the One who has eternal life can be the source of life. That can only be God Almighty. Giving life to all beings, creating them from nothing, and surrounding them with the proper conditions for them to live—only God can do that, because He has infinite power. Everything happens as He wishes."

Zippy said, "You're right! When a dry seed comes back to life, it shows that there is life after death, too." Plump Pigeon explained, "Creating something from nothing is easy for God the Almighty. Nothing is hard for Him. God can bring creatures back to life, just as He first created them from nothing." Zippy said, "You're right, Plump Pigeon. God is the Ruler,

the Director, who rules His creation with order and balance."
Chirpy had learned many beautiful and important things again, and he was very pleased.

Now Zippy went off to pick some walnuts. Chirpy and Plump Pigeon waited for Chirpy's mother to come home. They decided they would visit Greeny later.

After a while, Chirpy's mother arrived. She was carrying a lot of seeds in her beak. Laughing, Plump Pigeon said to Chirpy, "After eating all those non-living foods, you'll become more alive, won't you?"

Chirpy smiled. He thought that what Plump Pigeon had said was very meaningful. He said to himself, "God is the Giver of Life and life continues as He wishes."

THE LORD OF THE UNIVERSE

The evening before, the rain had refreshed the earth. Greeny's surroundings had become fresh, green, and lovely. It was as if the flowers in all their different colors were competing in beauty. Poppies, tulips, violets, daisies—there were so many natural beauties to see on Shepherd's Hill.

Greeny was no longer a little pine tree. He and his friends had grown taller with every passing day. In the same way, the flowers on the hillside around him had grown too. They had become a big family. Everything was wonderful.

That day Greeny had a long chat with Dragonfly. Greeny liked Dragonfly's name very much. Towards evening, just after Dragonfly had flown away, Chirpy and Plump Pigeon arrived. Greeny was very happy to see two more of his friends. "Welcome," said Greeny. "You know, you guys can perch on my branches from now on because I'm big enough to hold your weight now."

Carefully, the two birds perched on Greeny. They had also noticed the changes that had been taking place around him. Plump Pigeon said, "Shepherd's Hill has become a very beautiful place."

"Yes, it has become like the Garden of Paradise," he agreed. "That's thanks to Brother Cloud. He has never left us without water. He said that he's just following his orders."

"Who is giving his orders?" asked one of the daisies in the grass around Greeny. Everybody looked at the daisy,

surprised. "Why, God, of course!" said Greeny.

They had answered such questions several times before, but the daisy was so young that it was normal for her not to know the answer. "Yes, you're right, Greeny," agreed Plump Pigeon. But now little Daisy asked, "There are so many living beings everywhere in the world, and the world is very big. How can God manage all of those beings? Wouldn't it be easier if there were more than one creator?"

Everybody was shocked by her question. There was a short silence, and then they all responded together: "Of course not!" Little Daisy was startled. Her face became suddenly pale. "Did I say something wrong?" she asked, her big head trembling on her little stalk.

Plump Pigeon realized that the little daisy was frightened. He made his voice as gentle as possible. "Yes, Daisy. You did say something very wrong, but it's just because you don't know the truth yet."

"So do you mean that there is only one creator who is managing both the earth and the heavens?" asked the daisy.

Plump Pigeon hardly knew how to start. He wanted to explain it in a way that would be easy for the little daisy to understand. He asked Greeny whether he could explain it easily or not. "I don't think so," said Greeny. "But I saw Wise Rabbit a few minutes ago. My mother says Wise Rabbit knows a lot about everything. I guess she might answer this question in the best way. Let me call Wise Rabbit."

Greeny swayed his branches and rustled his needles, and a few minutes later Wise Rabbit arrived. "Did you call me, Greeny?" she asked. They told Wise Rabbit about little Daisy's questions. "Oh, don't worry," she said. "I think I can explain this very well to her with God's help." Then Wise Rabbit said to all of them, "Think of the cars that humans travel about in. Tell me, how many drivers are there in a car?" Greeny answered, "As far as I can make out, there is only one."

"That's right," said Wise Rabbit. "There's only one. What do you suppose would happen if a car had two drivers?"

"Then there should be two steering wheels," said Greeny.

"Let's suppose that there are two steering wheels," said Rabbit. Plump Pigeon immediately grasped what Wise Rabbit was trying to say. "I guess the car would be swerving and crashing all over the place if there were two steering wheels," he said. Two humans cannot drive one car at the same time."

Then Wise Rabbit asked another question. "Tell me, how many mayors are there in a town where humans live?"

"Only one," said Plump Pigeon, who had visited lots of towns where humans lived and listened to humans talking. "And what would happen if a town had two mayors?" asked Rabbit. "There would probably be lots of arguments and problems," said Plump Pigeon. "People wouldn't know who to obey or what to do."

"That's right," said Wise Rabbit. She turned to little Daisy. "How many presidents do you think there are in a country?" she asked. "Only one?" guessed Daisy. "Right," said rabbit. "So, Daisy, what do you think would happen if there were more than one president?"

"I guess everything would be in a mess," said Daisy. "Humans wouldn't know who to listen to. There would be no peace. The country would fall apart."

"That's right," said Rabbit, "and now let me ask you another question, little Daisy. What would happen if there were more than one God? Think of the earth and also the thousands of beings in the sky." Everybody was looking at little Daisy. Now she could understand that it was not logical to think that there might be more than one God. In a shy voice, she said, "I see, Wise Rabbit. My question was silly."

"Don't be sad," said Wise Rabbit. "Now you understand why one of the Names of our Lord is Ahad. That means that He is God, the One and Only. None is like Him."

Plump Pigeon felt more comfortable now. "Oh, thank you, Wise Rabbit. You explained it very well. There cannot be two mayors in a town or two presidents in a country. The Eternal Owner of this universe is God, the One. His power has no limits. He doesn't need a partner or any assistant. Nobody is like Him and He is like nobody."

114

Chirpy looked around. Evening was falling. "I think I'd better go, or my mother will be worried," he said to Plump Pigeon. Then he turned to the Wise Rabbit. "I enjoyed this conversation a lot. Thank you very much. Now I see why they call you wise. We live in the grove over there. We would be very happy if you visited us. Then we could learn more from you."

Another beautiful day was almost over. The beautiful face of the moon shone in the sky. It was a sign that it was time to leave. So Chirpy and Plump Pigeon said goodbye to their friends and flew off. Greeny waved to them. Then he said to Wise Rabbit, "Why don't you stay here with me tonight. We can talk some more."

"Thank you," said Wise Rabbit, "but my children will be waiting for their bedtime story. I really must go."

With that she said goodnight to Greeny and hopped off to her home. Greeny wished goodnight to little Daisy, whose question had started all the interesting talk, and happily fell asleep for the night.

THE LOVER AND THE BELOVED

Time was passing very fast. Chirpy was not as small as he used to be. His friendship with Greeny was getting closer and closer. He had made other friends, too. They were having important conversations about the Names of God. They were trying to grasp the meanings of the Names.

Chirpy counted on his feathers as he was talking to himself. "How many Names have we learned so far? I guess there must be many more. Wise Rabbit told us that all these Names are called the Beautiful Names of God." As he had learned the Beautiful Names that he knew so far, he had started to love God

more and more, and he said the Names often. "My dear Lord, I love You so much that I cannot really put it into words," he prayed. "Please love me, too! I want to be loved by You."

While he was deep in thought, Chirpy suddenly noticed a buzzing noise. It was a honeybee. He was collecting nectar from the flowers. "Hey, brother," called Chirpy. "You look tired. If you like, you can come and have a rest here." The honey bee hesitated. "I am sorry," he said slowly, "but my mother told me not to get too close to birds."

"Oh, don't worry," said Chirpy. "I won't do you any harm, I promise."

The honeybee was very tired. He thought that Chirpy's nest looked like a very good place to have a rest, and Chirpy did not seem to be a bad guy. "OK. I'm coming," said the honeybee.

"Welcome, brother," said his new bird friend. "My name is Chirpy. I think you have been working very hard today."

"Yes, I have, but I need to work harder," said the honeybee.

"Why?"

"Well, we have a very short life and we have a lot to do. You know we make a lot of honey."

"Yes," said Chirpy. "How do you make all that honey? Can you really eat that much?"

"Of course we don't eat all of it ourselves," laughed the honeybee. "We make honey mostly for human beings. They like honey very much."

Chirpy was very surprised. He wanted to ask why bees cared for human beings, but he thought that it might not be right to ask. He decided to ask another question instead. "How did you learn to make honey? I guess it must be quite hard to make," he said.

"Yes, it is hard," answered the honeybee. "But for the One who taught us, nothing is hard. Our Lord inspires us to make honey."

"How does that inspiration come to you?" asked Chirpy.

"First our Lord inspires us to build our homes in mountains, trees and beehives and to eat a variety of food," said the honeybee. "Then He wills us to go wherever He directs. Then, by His order, we build honeycombs and make honey."

"Is there any guide about the amount of honey you make?" asked Chirpy.

"Of course," said the honeybee. "The honeycombs we build have cells in the shape of hexagons. A hexagon shape, you

might know, has six equal sides. Then we collect nectar from thousands of flowers to make the honey that we store in the cells in the honeycomb."

"Are the flowers where you collect nectar always close to you?"

"No. Some of them are close, but some are tens of miles away."

"So you also go to places far away from here?"

"Yes, we do."

"Don't you ever get lost?"

"Our flight route is recorded in our brain. So we never get lost."

"Don't you get tired?"

"Yes, but we love our work. Is there anything better in the world than helping human beings?"

Chirpy was still curious about that. Why did bees care for human beings? He decided to ask the question in a different way. "Do you make honey just for human beings?" he said.

"No," said the little bee. "We also eat it ourselves, but we give most of it to human beings."

"Why?"

"Well, one of the Names of God is al-Wadud. That means that He is the All-Loving. He is the One who is loved the most. He is the One who loves human beings. He cares for them at every stage of their lives. One of the blessings He provides for human beings is honey. He loves His loyal servants, and they can have God's love and friendship in this life. He also makes others love the ones He loves."

"Now I see," said Chirpy thoughtfully. "So, do you think it's worth making honey?"

"I think it is," said the honeybee.

"It's clear that God loves human beings very much, and it's impossible not to love what He loves."

"You know," the honeybee added, "everybody wonders about bees. I can tell you more about us if you like."

"Actually, I'm really curious about your life," said Chirpy. "I don't mean to be rude, but how do you manage to do all those complicated tasks when you have such a small head?"

"I think you should think of the One who inspires us instead of thinking of us bees. It's God Almighty who changes the essence of flowers into honey in our bodies. There is no difference between the honey that we make today and the honey our ancestors made in the first days of Earth. We've been the experts at this job since bees were created for the first time."

"I've heard that honey also works as a medicine. Is that true?"

"Yes, it's good for a lot of illnesses," said the honeybee in a pleased kind of way.

Chirpy remembered that one of the Names of God is the Healer.

He started another prayer. "You are always sending blessings on us, my dear Lord! You command the sun to give us heat and light. You command the clouds to give us rain. You make living beings love each other. You inspire beings which cannot think to do very clever things.

All praises be to You. You are al-Wadud, the One who loves and the One who is loved the most. I love you very much."

The bee listened to Chirpy with admiration. He was happy he had made such a good friend. He decided he would like to visit him very often. He said, "I like you so much, Chirpy. I'll visit you again if I can."

"I'd be very happy if you visit me again," said Chirpy. "I'd also like to learn about your work in the beehive. Would you tell me?"

"Certainly. It will be my pleasure. It will be another chance for us to remember our Lord and get His eternal love," said the honeybee over his shoulder as he flew off to his work again. Waving goodbye to the honeybee, Chirpy exclaimed, "My Lord, how beautiful You are and how wonderful it is to love and to be loved!"